Praise for Anca Vlasopolos' previous books

Walking Toward Solstice
"Anca Vlasopolos' poems in *Walking Toward Solstice* are a battle cry—bracing, powerful, and luminous. With spare eloquence, she evokes a world that's turned cruel and unforgiving. Her poetry is as distinct as her fingerprints."
        Patricia Abbott, author of *Monkey Justice and Other Stories* and *Concrete Angel*

Penguins in a Warming World
"The poems in *Penguins in a Warming World* move by narrative and association, through science and religion, from St. Clair Street in Detroit to a quiet fountain in a mosque of the medieval city on Rhodes, to the beasts of the field and the bugs that crawl on them."
        Keith Taylor, poet, short-story writer, and winner of the Keeley and Sherrard Award for translation of Costas Karyotakis's poetry

No Return Address
"'How and where can I rewrite the history of anonymous women?' asks Vlasopolos in *No Return Address*. The memoir itself, the 'very act of writing without fear,' is the answer to this question. Reflecting on her mother's courage in leaving all she had known and bringing her out of Rumania, Anca Vlasopolos writes exactly that history."
        Robert Eaglestone, author of *The Holocaust and the Postmodern* in *TLS* (*The Times Literary Supplement*), January 26, 2001.

Cartographies of Scale (and Wing)

Anca Vlasopolos

Also by Anca Vlasopolos

Poetry

Walking Toward Solstice. Norman, OK: Mongrel Empire Press, 2012.

Penguins in a Warming World. Princeton: Ragged Sky Press, 2007.

Sidereal and Closer Griefs. (26-poem chapbook) *Origami Condom*, http://origamicondom.org/Chapbooks/Vlasopolos.01.pdf (May 2008).

Through the Straits, At Large. Detroit: Ridgeway Press, 1997.

The Evidence of Spring. Detroit: Ridgeway Press, 1989.

Fiction, Memoir, Scholarship

The New Bedford Samurai. Kingsport, TN: Twilight Times Books, , September 2007.

No Return Address: A Memoir of Displacement. New York: Columbia University Press, 2000.

Missing Members. Detroit: Corridors Press, 1990.

The Symbolic Method of Coleridge, Baudelaire, and Yeats. Detroit: Wayne State University Press, 1983.

Cartographies of Scale (and Wing)

Poems by

Anca Vlasopolos

Avignon Press
Newport Beach, California

Copyright 2015 Anca Vlasopolos

All rights reserved. No part of this book may be reproduced without written permission from the author or publisher except by a reviewer or critic who may use brief excerpts to be printed in a book, magazine, newspaper or online source for purposes of critical articles or reviews.

Vlasopolos, Anca
Cartographies of Scale (and Wing)

Poetry — Birds — Map-Making — Migration — Cartography — Ecology

Cover Art: *Grunge World* by Zoya Fedrova | Dreamstime.com with superimposed *Ducks in Flight* from *Friends in Feathers and Fur, and Other Neighbors* by James Johonnot (1823-1888)

ISBN: 978-0-9962920-0-9

Avignon Press
Newport Beach, California, USA

Acknowledgments

I thank Wayne State University, its Department of English, and its Humanities Center for their support in giving me the time to complete this book. My writers' group, my older daughter, Olivia V. Ambrogio, and my husband and technical support, Anthony Ambrogio, have my heartfelt thanks for their help and encouragement while the work was in progress.

The following poems appeared in literary journals and anthologies, and I thank the editors for their usually unpaid labors of love in promoting poetry:

"At Grass Level." *My Vision, Your Voice: An Artistic Duet*. Ed. Suzanne Scarfone. 2012.

"Duck Economies." *Jellyfish Whispers*. 2013.

"Each Life." *Public Republic*. 2009.

"Finch Speaks from Fallow Field." *Limestone*. 1999.

"Mere Forage." *Great Lakes Poetry Project*. Ed. Blake Walters. 2013.

"Molting." *Poets.net*. 2009.

"No Multitudes." *Muddy River Review*. 2011.

"Perfectly Clear." *My Vision, Your Voice: An Artistic Duet*. Ed. Suzanne Scarfone. 2012.

"Warming Still." *The Externalist*. 2007.

Illustrations

Bird in Flight (title page) from *St. Nicholas Magazine for Boys and Girls, Vol. 5, September 1878, No. 11.*

Cartographer's Tools (p. 1) From *Tales Worth Telling, Traveller's Adventures by Sea and Land*, published by Munroe and Francis & C.S. Francis & Co., 1852.

World Map on Double Cordiform Projection, 1538 (p. 7) This world map on two sheets is an early work of the famous Flemish cartographer Gerardus Mercator (1512-1594). His solution to the problem of accurately conveying the earth's sphere in two dimensions, as used here in a double heart-shaped projection, preceded his eventual use of a series of plates to portray a single projection of the world in two dimensions, which he accomplished in 1569 with his famous "Mercator Projection." (picture: Wikimedia)

Ducks in Flight (p. 17) from *Friends in Feathers and Fur, and Other Neighbors* by James Johonnot (1823-1888).

Damselfly (p. 27) Drawing by Olivia V. Ambrogio, a writer and biologist by training who currently works in science communication/outreach. Her writing and art can be found on her blogs, *Beasts in a Populous City* and *Sensing Wonder.*

Bird With a Nest (p. 63) from *Nellie's Housekeeping Little Sunbeams Series, 1882*, by Joanna H. Mathews.

Table of Contents

1. MAKING MAPS 1
   Edge Gilt 4
   Campus Map 5
   Lost Bearings 6
2. VISIONARIES OF THE MAPS 7
   Mercator Makes Maps 10
   Map Collections 13
   Dead Reckoning 14
   Celestial Mechanics 15
3. MIGRATION WITHOUT MAPS 17
   Scoring Scars: Crossing the Bering Straits down to Tierra del Fuego 20
   Polynesians Setting Out for Unknown Lands 22
   That and We 23
   Sailing to Lampedusa 24
4. NAVIGATION BY UNKNOWN MAPS 27
   Vacant Skies 30
   No Multitudes 32
   Beyond the Eye and Ear 34
   Seabirds Continue to Wash Up on Oregon Coast 35
   At Water's Edge 36
   ID Denied 37
   Finch Speaks in Fallow Fields 38
   Each Life 39

At Sixty-One 40

Spring in Seattle After Chernobyl, 1986 41

Sighting 42

Molting 43

Memo: It's Time 44

Mundane Predation 45

Duck Economies 46

Warming Still 48

Mechanics of Uplift 49

Dragonflies Don't Tell 50

Turn 51

Night Arrows 52

Singular Reprieve 53

Empty Spoons 54

Unfathomed Altruism 56

Seams Undone 57

April Benignity 58

Layers 59

Ahodori 60

Between 62

5. TRYING TO STAY IN PLACE 63

Moon Snail Trespass 66

Mere Forage 67

Beaching 68

Postmodern Threats 70

From the Reviled Bird's View 72

Then They Came Out 74

Highway Song 75

Open Ends 76

Bird Secrets 78

Perfectly Clear 80

Rest Stop 81

At Grass Level 82

Mantis Shrimp 83

Medusas 84

Sparrow's Fall 85

Late Disturbances 86

Heralds 87

Wind Effect 88

We Decree 89

So Much Depends 90

ABOUT THE AUTHOR 91

1. MAKING MAPS

"Benevolent Reader, take pleasure in our labors and whenever something is lacking in either map or description, bear in mind that a mistake is easily made when describing a place one has never seen and that forgiveness is nowhere more appropriate than here."

Atlas Maior (1665), Joan Blaeu

"Maps are guilty of distortion . . . . Maps are only human, after all."

Dava Sobel (2013

Edge Gilt

each map shows intent
someone(s)'s wanting to know to mark   to challenge
        smoothe successors' progress   draw puff-cheeked gods and
                cannibals   make it eye-popping pretty

        in postmodern jaundiced eye
all guilty
        hiding   blanking details   too intricate for the large picture
                global erasing local ways

civilizations
        we keep finding because we won't believe
like a mousse layer cake
        brown/white/beige/spongy/deliciously compact/perfect in texture
                all oozing sweet-salt blood
                      upon and under crusts of hardened lava flows
                          mud sediments

each makes maps
to place on bark   parchment   sheepskin   cave wall
        reaches of habitation
                under a shifting but immutable firmament
eager to pass that image on and on
        through human fires: Carthage Alexandria
                inflamed heathens' Christians'   Jews'   Muslims'
        fascists'   communists'   evangelicals'   just small minds'

till we
        each time
                from mere stories   rumors   sailors' yarns
set out   again
to patch up
        our altering sphere

Campus Map

        not a google or mapquest
this
        etched along neurons   synapses
        other labyrinths of that organ
        that   like the others
        begins its sloughing off
from the time I embarked toward knowing
        like my Ithacan ancestor
        though unlike him not forced to it but eager to see sails fill with wind
                since for me there was no throne to grow cold
to now as I edge toward redundancy
this campus
has shifted
from
        left-over gardens   homes here
        in the city's innards
        land gobbled up by the other
                city of knowledge pumped up
                      with endless youth flow—War's-end ecstasies
        where old viburnums still skirting the library
                hid   fed   ovenbird and thrush
        where the yews' poisoned—for us—jewels fed catbird   cardinal
        huge cottonwood held kestrel camouflaging razors
to
what we now have made   paved   manicured   monocultured
        overtrod   electronified
all but this dusty candy-wrapper-strewn
corner of parking lot
where
chipping white throat   white crown   song
still flit in and out of broken   forgotten   fighting   forsythias   conifers

Lost Bearings

no matter how sharp the app
how good the guide
they will not look
as pictured   drawn   photographed
see this familiar woodpecker
        black-and-white striations more elegant than any evening dress
            now veiled in citron

this afternoon
        bathed in honey light
turns all to gold dust
glamour fills my eyes

cobwebs swim freely
        through meadow air
        tied to no spinning
        nor the spinner

yet I get caught
hair   hands   binoculars
a gulliver among
        invisible lilliputians

        binding me fast
        to this loud silence
        these flitting shape-shifters
        this lingering late-fall disquiet

2. VISIONARIES OF THE MAPS

Born in Flanders in 1512, Gerardus Mercator developed the globe mapping that we still use today, called the "Mercator projection." He accurately projected the globe onto a flat surface, but his great contribution was that he created a formula through which longitude and latitude lines are at right angles to each other.

His map of the world, published in 1569, revolutionized navigation. Navigators could henceforth plot a route between any two places on the map using a straight line, and then follow that route without having to adjust their compasses.

Mercator's straightening of longitude and latitude lines, and the spaces in between, had the effect of distorting distances and places. Greenland and the Antarctica appear much larger through the mercatorian projection than they are. Mercator was also the first person to use the word "atlas" to refer to a collection of maps bound together in a book.

* * *

Born in Salem, Massachusetts, in 1773, Nathaniel Bowditch grew up alongside the American Revolution. He was self-educated and tutored by townsmen who noticed his genius for mathematics. He taught himself calculus in order to read Newton's *Principia*, in which he discovered two errors, for which he was boxed on the ears by a Harvard professor for his audacity in challenging Newton.

He made four sea voyages between 1795 and 1799, the last as captain, during which he perfected his tables for calculating the exact position of a ship on oceans using coordinates that could be read and understood by ordinary sailors, thereby undermining the "monarch of the seas" captaincy that made slaves of the crew on vessels. In March 1798, he married Elizabeth Boardman, who died seven months later, while he was at sea.

His contributions to navigation were such that at the time of his death, in 1838, flags were lowered in harbors of thirty-seven countries.

Mercator Makes Maps

like the good things we take for ourselves
they traveled with us
from blessed isles
where all you do
is stand
and fruit falls
for your taking
unless
a dragon
comes from the underbrush
for her ripe meal—
you standing

we now toss them casually
into the lunch box
glowing in a bowl

and every year
in one or another class
of small prisoners
teachers
assign
the orange
to stand in
for our ellipse

children dutifully
peel with small
clumsy fingers
attach to cardboard sheets
these vivid fragrant
rinds
still trying
to resist
the flattening

you
Gerardus Mercator
in fogs of Flanderland
did you hold oranges

do we know
what prompted
your geometric genius

was it a grape
you squashed
under
as you walked
pondering
the sphere

an apple
blushing rind
after you'd done
skinning
with sharp knife
letting it coil
upon a damask tablecloth

did you
like Archimedes
unmindful
of all else
run
back
with trembling fingers
unclothe
nail to the wall
the shimmering
dress
of this
our
little globe
now
emptied of loving roundness

left
naked
to probing
anatomizing
yet
to come

Map Collections

Gerardus
you called maps bound
atlas

struck with cleverness
and classic learning
forgetting

defeated Titan
bracing
against the pregnant weight

this rounded sack
its skin of gravity
holding in

the generative seas
masses of stone
and ground-down rock

you straightened longitude's
imaginary ribs defining this our breast
enlarged to monster shape Greenland

Antarctica
riding on widened
latitudes

the point?
that we should get in line
from here to there

forgetting
the tilt the sway
this bucking errant planet

Dead Reckoning

      to Nathaniel Bowditch, author of the *American Practical Navigator**

      hard against my skull
planks speak
      of woods snagging clouds
            storm-worried sails
      those mornings when sweet thrush pierces heartache's armor
but night here on largest ocean is a crystal bowl over swells as gentle as babe's
                              sleep

I cannot
      take time to love these myriad lit worlds calling to my eyes
I must
I must turn on my side

take out sextant
scribble in luminous dark
my inscriptions (*the pencil marks and lines should not be needlessly numerous, heavy, or long*)

triangulate (*longitude equal to the hour angle of the celestial body from the prime meridian*)

then leave this languorous air
      that licks my fingertips as if I stroked the siren's skin
           pencil slipping   rolling not far off
for foul below-deck
and my calculations
      altitude   *azimuth tables so precise*

each simple sailor
      no longer in thrall to "monarchs" of the seas
will find
      rid of all doubt
true bearing

* Italics in this poem and the next are quotations from Bowditch's *American Practical Navigator* (1804)

Celestial Mechanics

night sky battened down
          impenetrable tarp
Marblehead bay
        teeth bared
                waiting for one minute miscalculation

"Every man among you's read the chart, knows the course?"

each assent voiced from faces blurred   whiteout   fog

on land
        ship rose a moment between blasts
            vanished
Salem men shook their heads
        knowing the morrow—Christmas—would find them dragging bodies out

no lights of merriment to guide her in
Puritan Eve and Day of Savior's birth reduced to only the other side
        of coin   sorrowing his earthly end   no joy to greet his coming

Bowditch saw all his men off safe
        in cottonwool walked to his house
        shivered the night long among deserted finery
            his heart's darling dead
                less than a year after the wedding day
mother three brothers two sisters baby long cold beneath the earth
        bride   all   fallen to that cough that tattered lungs as if fine
                      silk left in the sun

Christmas day
        familiar round face peering from the gloom
"Nate, is that you? Saved? Speak! Or I shall think you a specter come to upbraid our cowardice,
        none brave enough to push out in pea soup!"

    God's immutable laws governing celestial bodies and pure mathematics
    trump nature's worst

but he said
"'Tis I, in flesh and blood. All men from *The Eurydice* live."

3. MIGRATION WITHOUT MAPS

"Migrations have occurred throughout human history, beginning with the movements of the first human groups from their origins in East Africa to their current location in the world."

National Geographic

Nisan brings the matzoh moon
urging buds to open, urging
minds to fling their gates
wide on the night we become
slaves and then march out
to freedom past lintels
smeared with blood.

The Crooked Inheritance, Marge Piercy

... the great ships ... wandered the oceans
. . . .

... they sliced the pages of tropical seas in silence,
Divided by height, category, and class, just like our societies and hotels.
Down below poor emigrants played cards, and no one won.

Eternal Enemies, Adam Sagajewski

Scoring Scars: Crossing the Bering Straits down to Tierra del Fuego

what would so spur them   arrowpoint sharp
           from eyeball-shattering cold where lids turn to slits
     to cross uncertain ice to an uncertain end
if one there be

caribou   furred skeletons
had left without a backward glance
     never to return
          even their skin and bones   gone

birds no bigger than a snowball
went
came back with the thaws

     perhaps
these humans too could perch on anything
     off ground from the scythe

     filing across
         babes packed snug on backs
         sleds like snails carrying their all
they traversed white world to white world
     over green-white chasms

ice at times gave way
mother daughter child
     too heavy for ice floe
         mother pushing
     daughter grandchild
         into future
         clement or pitiless
     as fate would have it

about half made it
     some to stay in snow's kingdom
         whose ravenous rules they already knew
     but this side

caribou
had become a little more substantial
        than the other world's ghostly mockeries

others passed
        one land and another
                from ice to rain to sun to scorching light
        leaving those who no longer could or would
        leaving them to settle on plains   in caves   in sheltered valleys
        leaving them to plunder   burn   kill
        for no matter where we come from
        we remain true to our humanness
passed down
to where the stars
        had turned
                now pointing to a world
they'd be first   perhaps   first they would always claim
        to begin
                to know

Polynesians Setting Out for Unknown Lands

children shrivel   flowers just opening to burning sun
     cisterns empty
we wait and wait for rain

they come with the rains
     cawing through nights and days
on rocks hanging over waters   rocks white with birdshit

     when the rains stop
birds colored black white pink blue rise   leave behind
puffballs of soot bigger than themselves

one puffball jumps   floats on the wind
comes calling for the others
they too take the leap   fade into skysea

like them   o dying ones
we must put out to sea and trust
we too will find   along the paths they mark

another land   green   watery
where we release our game rats
and begin   anew   children making memories of us

That and We

a well-kept path through woods a stone's throw
                                  from a four-lane street
but
         as i duck   twist ankles over tree roots covered up in mulch
                look up in moment's fear   around   as massive flights of geese
                          pass overhead alarmed
                                 with honks to wake the dead
        slap at myriad insects—even armored as i am these modern times—

      suddenly
i know exactly
how they felt
          no moment to gasp at jeweled double-winged azure dragonfly
                  fired epaulettes of shrilling blackbirds
since

every natural thing
seemed to conspire
     against progress
          space   light   their life

so each
    as they came
hacked
cut
marked
chopped
sank dead posts
bound
kept out

this
    pushy   fighting   choking
        ever   wanting
force

Sailing to Lampedusa

can you really stand on one shore and see across?
        rock of Gibraltar   smooth pocket havens of North Africa

those starting out on moonless nights
        having walked on cracked bleeding soles
              from Niger   through Mali   Algeria
surely pin their hopes
        like blindfolded children
            with fake tails in hand
                but even the kids will come upon something solider
        than these
        big-bellied women   some with toddler glued to hip
            in much-patched rubber rafts
        braving the wine-dark sewer of our excesses
on dreams   nothing but dreams

they crave this life of rich and flowing garbage
        where children will not eat grass and mud
        where
              yes
        they will be hunted
        but not cut down   raped with bayonets
        where if perchance a man be in their future
            he will not end in pieces strewn to scavengers

they cross
        like storks
            like cranes
                like swallows
        these tricky waters on leaky vessels
            so many foundering
            so many joining the chain of human bones
        that stretches across this sea and all of the Atlantic

this woman
                on pleasant coast of Spain
        eating church charity
        braiding spoiled girls' hair for candy bars for her own little ones

says
this is
 the better life
this is
a life

4. NAVIGATION BY UNKNOWN MAPS

"Migratory birds have a long history of defying scientific ideas about their capabilities."

National Wildlife magazine

"For millennia the seasonal appearance and disappearance of birds has been obvious to hunters and casual observers alike, . . . but where most of them went to or came from was a subject of great speculation."
The Wisdom of Birds, Tim Birkhead

Vacant Skies

        from that first bolt striking primordial soup
                      fusing chance strands
                              since we became
            "improbable, perfect, most unstable"
we
        needing at first   light   to feed on
have looked
up

        even after
                as some of us dragged ourselves into weightier matter
                as some began to feed on us   not just on light
we
could not help
our impulse
to look
up

        on shores of blood-dark seas
                they looked as skies darkened at equinox
                      myriad cries above
                              overnight landings that broke trees

how could they not seek answers in the blood   guts   spilled feathers
        holding secrets of origin   undreamed of voyages   and what's to come

how could they not look up to know the coming
                to watch in dread the slow but sure withdrawal
                      of Demeter's good will

what's left for us?
        flung black triangles like tiny chattering warheads
                pretending migration
                      settling on treetops whence to mock our ring tones
        here not so much
                there on privileged shores   on hilltops

                        winged nations
                                    passing
briefly
telling us
            this you have deliberately lost   this
you can only see as you look up
                        on privileged shores   on the rare hilltops

No Multitudes

no more clapping clouds
blowing away daylight

now
swallows' exit
registers
for those who even notice
as mere absence

few flocks gather
thick enough
like passenger pigeons'
to crack the roosting branch
to give
soil
what soil needs
offending our sense
of covert emptying

we now want to go after
populations out of control
cormorants   geese   gulls   vultures
we want to prize these
as precious because rare
the perverse gourmet's whale steak
collectors' single and last egg

here at lakeside   empty of its handful
one "common" tern cries out
unanswered
one row of geese—seven birds in all—
shears the blue
settles with splashes creaks

silent the helicopter
dragonflies
practice
for their
uncharted as yet   by us
flight

Beyond the Eye and Ear

we expect gradual decline
downhill is fast yet
it's a motion we apprehend

but this
one evening to the next
one dawn
one lowering of lids

take for instance
cicadas rubbing so hard
we wonder they don't set
trees on fire
so gone
whole canopies seem
startled by bird screams

egrets like exclamation points
punctuating a negative print
that suddenly empty loses its syntax

we chide ourselves
how inattentive our ear our eye
that these departures went undetected

but change comes
as fast
as that drop of lid
that unalterable
unvapored
luminous
mirror
before shut lips

Seabirds Continue to Wash Up on Oregon Coast

no tree has yet answered to the name
no plant
unless you count those housemates
who learn to syncopate their symmetries
to the imprisoned anguish
inside Mozart's giddy violins

so now these birds
a half a world away
from mammals who
        through human all-too-human fancy
named them
        these rhinoceros
        of open waters
        diving two hundred feet to scoop
        just a small sardine

these formal black-white auklets
attending their acrobatic balls
show up
in droves
on coasts
washed up
drowned
tuxedoed
for their own funeral
as if
in solidarity
a half a world away
with hornèd beasts
who too
are

gone tomorrow

At Water's Edge

three monarchs ride
        this September afternoon   on uncertain air
rise on warm breaths of waning sun
hover
zig-zag away from icy fingers   northern winds   for lower ground

tell me
        outside Dubuque   on the magic tree you showed me
            (my only time with you)
        is there this year a veil of butterflies   making tree quiver   bloom
            stopped to soak up
            enough of summer's lingering heat
            to take them the unimaginable miles
            all the way to the valley below our heaving border
                their secret wintering grounds

        this year bereft of butterflies
these three
        tatters
are left from plenty's tapestry
                frayed by tooth and claw of our mindlessness
            worried to near-death

ID Denied

four ice floes   no
small icebergs   maybe iceberg tips
     moving west   in blinding line of winter sunset

i wanted more
raise your heads   *raise them!*

how could i count them   account for them   on e-bird in bird journal

when marks of species
     orange beak—mute   black beak—trumpeter
          black with a touch of orange—tundra
pulled at underwater weeds
perhaps found minnows still
     in that clay-churning water

RAISE THEM! i shouted like the idiot i am
only to see them speed ever toward light
     busy   indifferent   navigating through these so dark waters
          in symmetry and perfect equidistance of companionship
leaving me and my good binoculars
     impotent
          on frozen shore

Finch Speaks in Fallow Fields

the flapping water like sheets hung out to dry
in wind
clouds wooly low
undersides of unshorn sheep
stupidly ready to drop over the cliff
and i?
see-saw on slender stems
jacob's ladders
stick to rough rude tops of coneflowers
cling tight to spaces between mean thorns
to pluck sheen from these
these purple only purples
that paint me from inside
gaudy
parisian elegant
eye-poking
black and citron

Each Life

on October 9, 5769,
Atonement Day,
the thrush stood in the middle of Lakeland
        the street that takes me
        where I face St. Clair
        to cast once more
        my bread upon its waters

stood there
        unmoving
        ready to be hit
        by passing cars

let me scoop up its olive body
        weight no more than
        fallen leaf
        pink legs propped against my palms
        eyes blinking at the sun
        as if stunned by this autumnal brilliance

        as I peered to look for signs
        of hurt
it lifted itself in one swift motion
        from cradling hands
flew sure and straight
        for shelter under shrubs

minuscule mortal god I
        for just this day
        this hour
        this minute
held the power
        to write
        this migrant
        in the Book of Life

At Sixty-One

that birthday morning as i rejoiced to spot
breast freckles
bobbing red tail
i had no inkling

later the lake fumed
platinum
unaffordably rich gray

the sheltered seawall corner
"park your wagons here"
now lashed by whips of algae-wielding waves

in beechen green
susurrations almost insect-like
kinglets fatly sporting a foot away

i had no inkling
of that bang at dusk
thrush on its back

thrush in my hand
breathing red
eyes slowly closing

heart going two beats
after lowered lids
beak leaving a thin mark

as vivid on my wrist
as my life's blood

Spring in Seattle After Chernobyl, 1986

It happened, we don't know exactly, there on the edge
          of Europe, Asia. Why
do we avoid looking into this fine mist,
this harrowing sun in a sky of blood?
What do we fear from azaleas' scent
in a month mother's milk, in fall the proferred apple,
in a year the yearling trussed for the feast?

It happened over there, after all, and the clouds
and the air lifting themselves in heaves
round and round
should know better, should read down, should catch
on to barbed wire, armed guards, un/natural boundaries.

Yet this fine mist, this sun surgically scraping
against the horizon wall
are simply themselves
          and just here
no more

Sighting

first it was only a duskier sparrow framed
in the diamond wire of the cyclone fence
almost black and untidy in dim morning light

then as I looked ran for binoculars
it moved flew to the darker dark beneath
weeping crabs themselves beneath an overarching maple
there glowing as if dusted with radioactive powder

it is, I murmured to myself to make myself
believe
indigo bunting
another of my lone sightings like the humming bird
at the azalea bloom
like the pair of orioles chasing each other
through the lilac

sightings to raise eyebrows to make those
hearing me exchange knowing looks

that afternoon as I was telling my tall tale
it reappeared for three of us to see
the film in the camera put in with trembling hands
failing to catch
the telephoto lens just barely clicking
on what would be nothing but turquoise blur
against slate bark
nothing but drab words
nothing to show for
this fugitive through this our climate
not fresh not cool enough
to tempt repose

Molting

this winter says it has settled
for good
so that even now
late March we expect
more and more snow
mocking
a post-equinox sun

yet on the finch feeder
there's no denying
even if smiles still crack lips
that pathetic ridiculous
mix
of olive camouflage
starting to tatter
being pushed
aside

patches
bright-lemon yellow
opera black
struggling toward
dapper array
males on the make

Memo: It's Time

at dusk
clouds swept up in thin wisps
        like a woman's grey hair   escaping in the wind
sun shocked us
turned the lights off so early in the day

but   clearly
        in hieroglyphs with no Rosetta stone
a message did go out
        on that grey-rose board

        for
look
this morning grass
sports crowds of polka-dotted bodies
starlings like wind-up toys   up   down   up
        picking out grubs

crabapple
        winking vermillion
sways under frenzied flurried weight
        robins gorging   their own breasts flames
        in morning light

then
this very afternoon
emptiness
        at least as we can see
            though can we tell
            groundfeeders under cover
            poised raptor
                in feather pantaloons hiding
        scythes

Mundane Predation

petroleum rainbows dance off its sheen
        as it struts
throws yellow eye darts
        startling the smaller birds into rushed hops away

squawks   grunts   screeches
announce its vying with others of its kind
        for best of branches fattest grubs
                juiciest   others'   eggs

                yet when now a heap
        beneath widespread toes ending in lancet talons
        feathers' electric spark
        extinguished
you   feeder bully
do pull at the heartstrings

        as scimitar beak pulls and devours
        your viscera

                red as maple-bud husks
                falling   telling us
                      despite the sleet
spring
        this season of sex and death and sex
lands upon us
        no less impartially ferocious
                to those loveless   those dying
than this red-shouldered hawk

Duck Economies

technically i'm so inferior
binoculars
expensive   for me
still under $five hundred
scope only
child's toy
—reward
for thirty-five-years teaching

so i mostly
with frozen hands   watery eyes
guess
        at beak color
        wing tip
        ringed neck
know regal shapes of canvasbacks
can tell horns and clarinets of tundra swans

when home
i google
thinking luminous close-ups
will vivify
my fading visual snaps

among the photos
of these serenes
—illusionists on lake skin—
one microsecond caught in lenses' round
next arching
vanished as if they'd never been

i see shots
        of children triumphant
        high-tech guns slung over shoulders

holding aloft
        dogs's jaws clamped on
lifeless bodies

see carcasses
accompanied
by game cooking tips

Warming Still

this summer men pretending to own the world meet
to carve it up according to specs drawn by their puppeteers
outside mothers howl for children clobbered
hair yanked out
air made vicious with gas to make you weep

we've seen this stuff before
so many times before

the planet imperceptibly revolves its blues and greens
and pictures from the dark we only can imagine
show us smaller patches of white caps
more green
more yellow where they haven't been

on the news sharks bite and eat a few of crowds
using the oceans as pleasure pools
the news tells us how to fight the sharks
a former lobbyist now government employee
to watch the industry for which she lobbied
says we've allowed the sharks to go unhunted
for too long

a ladybug lands on your neck and bites
        on your friend's hand and bites
        on your sister's knee and bites
this we have not yet seen
this perhaps we should
take as a sign

Mechanics of Uplift

        this late October
        so gray that trees blaze forth
        like fireplaces in a ghostly manse

        breaking the compact between sky
                —like blanket underside—
        and lake sighing its own gray impotence
a whirr
        mechanical
bursts
        as if a pedal boat submerged
        had on a sudden struck through water
V line of utter white
insolently cuts heavy air

only spots of black
        to make the white more startling
insult this monochrome day

        tips of those swanheads heading only
they know where

Dragonflies Don't Tell

        at the lakeside park
silence

well, no, a motorboat whines in the distance
rigging hits against metal masts like bell tongues
cicadas saw at the afternoon
        as if divorcing it from itself
            were their life's mission

lake   puckering under wind
stands   wallpaper in a dentist's office
     white gulls   white sails   white clouds
     on green-blue expanse
     houses obedient on a shore
     with disciplined trees   shrubs lawns

do dragonflies calculate   set aside
     this tiny time
         no swallows   warblers   migrant sparrows
to gather in translucent yellow flames
swarm by lakeside in rehearsal
     for grand migration
     a comet's shimmering tail
not one of us knows where

Turn

the not-yet-summer afternoon wears on
fool young robins in throw-back plumage flounder

        as do horn-eared grackles—
unhinged yellow beaks opened in obstinate demand

an elegant long-legged beetle arrayed in orange bolero over black tight gown
companionably ambles next to me on seawall

while a kingbird surveys us
        perched between wire barbs

this day of waiting for dire news
has turned

the woman who hates locusts—"dirty trees"—
converts   at least for me   for now

as I try to spot waxwings   — "good for birds?"—
        among those feathered leaves

cotton puffs that so sicken me
fall with such grace   benign sweet squall

that I cannot but love them
        harbingers of schoolchild freedom

            not far off from this abundant air
      swirling with calls   seedpods   honks   gnats' dance

      in offices with cold equipment
death is still   for now   on holiday

Night Arrows

blood
sturgeon
moon
leaves no
path
to herself
on these sullen
waters

already
dented
one day imperfect
how does she
draw
in end-of-summer dark
this creaking
V
gliding beneath first stars
portent
of apertures
or
shutters

Singular Reprieve

even the dog
this january thaw
feels mildness
seeks
among shattered bones
        of winter snow
green

we walk
        for me to see the lake
watch
        sun
        an aging star
        through vaselined lens
                of foggy exhalations from this moment of reprieve

        bassoons sounding off
        ghosts rising from the waves
male swans
        not in the least mute
've begun their spring contentions

        on open waters
flocks numberless
diving ducks wait
        as if for stoplight

—stay here
for the duration
—go now
while
the going's good

Empty Spoons

Chukotka   summer heat equals our early March highs

puffballs on toothpicks
            begin as soon as eggshell falls
                        to forage with their minute triangular beaks

Bangladesh
            Myanmar   for the winter
                        poverty strangled

a two-ounce bird
            an almost unicorn
                        we've made it nearly as rare
travels from uppermost Siberia
            along the Yellow Sea
                        to snares
                                    beach-long nets
            in exotic Myanmar
                        where egrets   herons are being hoped for

when your child
            swollen-bellied
shrivels before your eyes
a bird the size of child's fist
makes the day's catch
you urge your young
            to crunch each delicate bone
                        each tiny leg
you only wish
            its wondrous spoon-shaped beak
                        were luscious licorice

and you remember when granny made
            a trayful of these birds
but now you're lucky this morsel
came into an ever-emptier net

the piper
   the one not caught this winter
sees a world we have no eyes for
follows a track inscribed inside her
   for hundreds of centuries
      three thousand miles at least
her wings the span of child's hand
beat beat
she needs to land
      her wondrous beak
   to seek quiver of mollusk burying fast in sand
she stops
   caught between waves and dry earth

since
   gray ugly useless—to us—mudflats teeming with rich sea soup
     along the coast of Yellow Sea
are now abandoned concrete walls
   vanished hopes of ports
     bustling commerce
       prosperity

so neither birds
   three hundred in the world
nor humans
   blindly seething into ten billion teetering toward certain crash
have
   left
anything

Unfathomed Altruism

They are peaceful, serious creatures. They know the secrets of the sea, they don't bark....
—Gérard de Nerval

admit it. *i* must.

you only imagine them armored
on a platter
mayonnaise   baked potato   corn on the cob
always
drawn butter
                              when   if   you think of them

    in a file a mile long
        on many spindly legs
            under seas few of us even skim
they march
    in a caravan of thousands
        flashing blue   brown   moss colors
   past
      pearls spilled out of sockets
          riffling currents silently robbing broken chests
            charts floating into transparency
      myriad tentacles reaching   to make a meal   like us   of them
   toward?
      warmer waters for their young?
      colder so they won't overheat from ardors of coupling?
they march   undaunted   the lengths of coasts
   in single conga line
      a leader forging through bottom sands
they march
    one bringing up the rear   this one
the hero
    lookout
            lure
to keep the others safe
be the one
dressed
in red

Seams Undone

they come
    first
        like threads freed from a seam
    zigzagging across world's edge
    where water and sky touch
then ply as on the needle's point
    what's left

    just as you think
        at the end of your tube
        I've got you!—merganser   grebe   bufflehead   shoveler

enact their disappearance

they stay
    longer now
        until
the lake skates circles   solid   solider around them
    till
        not enough remains

then fly
    to waters still unglazed

but we?
    as we move inland
        from loosed oceans
    and inland   more
    to higher
        and higher
            ground
how
    and to what
we'll fly?

April Benignity

first day full spring and late
wood under me stays warm
lake silence already torn by motors

mergansers henna-tipped
        green-purple punks
and buffleheads
        stark black and white like men
        at dinner parties in forties' movies
tease sight

willows have bleached their tresses

wind nips
tries milk teeth on skin
but sun's hands
        a good masseur's
leave too warm a glow

everything living pushes shoves
trills for company
and
look
the bonaparte's gull
swims among the ducks
watches with equanimity their vanishings and poppings-up
in weird and perfect safety
of this kissing day

Layers

Sedimentation, that long Latinate sibilant, imagines itself horizontal. But look at the woods out the window—layer upon layer of green, light yellow, chartreuse like the heady brew the monks trap in their bottles (appellation controlée); the surprise of pinks and reds, not flowers, spring leaves, set against gray lichen pointing north. Layers to the horizon, sounds, echoes, trumpets. Yes, thrush's song does rinse and wring the ear, yes, Beethoven's chords for this fifth sound through thrush's song, and the swell of the thrush sounds in and under and through the great man's music, the great poet's song, the Narragansett potter's tool carving the pot, and you cannot hear it alone for it has been heard, now and always, by emperor and clown, and each time is thrush and symphony and words and woven clay and the call of triumph and life.

Ahodori

*for Hiroshi Hasegawa, their guardian**

he bears scars from beaks
    like our noses circulating blood
    sensitive beaks that smell
    feel
    compressions of water becoming
    myriad invertebrate shapes
    glow-pink with a drop
    of bubblegum blue tips
tearing at enemy hands
going for private parts
for these birds though young
are no longer as foolish
as once

he wipes his eyes with the blue bandana around his neck
his voice cracks
as he places the one thousandth
special
gold band
on the twig leg
of this puffed soot
overgrown
comical chick
these birds to whose life he has
wedded his life

and some years later from deck
observing nesting grounds
he recalls
how
chick released
he looked up
to see humpbacks joyfully
breach
and he says
the birds the whales

companions in travel
as they cross
Pacific magnitudes
the few whales few birds still poised on brink
salute each other's
returns

* Ahodori: Japanese for "fool birds," the vernacular for short-tailed, or Steller's, albatross

Between

hoops snapped
winter casket lies
        shivered on softening ground

from among cerulean squill
        risen   brave   against the frosts
        spreading such fragrance to make us wonder
                if we've stepped off our earthly paths

trout lilies peep
        mirrors to
                eye-bursting tiny suns
                these early warblers

        caught between gold and gold
we see this mortal world
        for one cosmic particle of time

crack
        open

5. TRYING TO STAY IN PLACE

"[T]here are so many factors that affect habitat selection that it may be quite rare for any single habitat to be truly optimal—and even rarer that such optimal conditions can be identified."

The Sibley Guide to Bird Life & Behavior, David Allen Sibley

"Once settled, the new arrivals often arranged menial jobs, and a place to sleep, for friends and relatives, most of them also illegal, who joined them from their hometowns."

"Cross Purposes," *Smithsonian Magazine* (June, 2005)

Moon Snail Trespass

low tide
waves tolerant
let eyes fix
on treasures

huge quahog half
sanded jingle so fine
the gliding sun
slows to lick its apricot

you stoop to grab
        for waves still suck and sing and lure
        toward depths
this spiraled sphere like glass-spun paper weight
you lift it out of water
you scream
and fast replace it in sea-covered sands

you went for
shell
instead
the living thing
nearly transparent
firm jelly
reached into nothing air from opening

and this (not) shell
        that you have seen
        and held
        even collected
                gray swirls tobacco palest rose
screams out
in violent black
outraged pink
I'm still here!

Mere Forage

in late spring over the cement slab dropped in the water
whenever the humans built this sea wall
they appeared
so evanescent so slim so small
as if someone had cut a winter's soggy leaf
to shreds
and threw it in the lake

on days of fury they were nowhere
        that is nowhere my eyes could see

in summer heat i stopped my voyeurism
the path to this small public access to the lake
too sunny to be borne

        in starting desolation of fewer-bird september
        today the water gently waved like sheets in breeze
        lit like a photograph made with mercury tints
the school (why do we name such gatherings to mirror our arrangements?)
was there again
this time
these gizzard shad
        dorosoma the ancients called them for their lance-like shapes
        centuries later called skipjack for their leaps
now grown to fingerlings
allow me microsecond glimpses of growing bodies
        the tell-tale beauty mark on silver so pale so polished
        no one even in lakeside mansions owns

they stick together still
knowing what i did not
that they
who gladden through seasons eyes tired of lake's emptiness
are mere "forage" if that
for what
we truly prize

Beaching

        I

blood like smoke curls out of my ears
i hurtle myself against the others
do not   do not   for once
follow
i am not leading to silver shoals
will not thread our way among the shifting floes
blind now i heave myself
      rocks sand shells
      shredding my underside
      this sheet of fire crackling
      my body
no longer see
just hear
explosions
even in these wrecked ears
only the breathing so easy
breathing
to make this end
stretch
as if from pole to pole

        II

pilot whales off the Carolinas
dolphins in the Florida Keys
nine manatees
one right whale, female,
one from a handful left in oceans of this world

      like ours
lungs long
      for breath
heart pumps
and pumps
      blood getting bluer
      with each spurt
      like ours

eyes
cloud
limbs
grow languid
body
falls
   for those fields of stillness

   unlike ours
tongue
cannot
will not
tell
what
they who so long ago shed our heaviness
know
of what
propels them
   so urgently toward
us

Postmodern Threats

> *Despite years of being trapped, shot, and poisoned, Coyotes have maintained their numbers and continue to increase in the East.*

it used to be
no doubt still is
the BLACKS from just across
the invisible barrier
us/them

the Yellow hordes—
if all the folks in China
jumped at once...

now what pursues us
is merely what we've done

shadows drying up
as when a car sweeps its clean swath
of light
chasing night briefly
away

jaws slack with famished desire
yellow eyes
bones under tan-red apparel
deliquescent

so they can flow
in and out of yards
our marked and guarded
property

take what some of us most cherish
small sweet and helpless dog
cat agile but not enough

we spin our horror tales
of these invaders come over
Great Lakes ice

like those who crossed from Asia
whom
we also
ruthlessly
displaced

From the Reviled Bird's View

After Eudora Welty's **Untitled** *New York Scape*

from my roost
under shelter of stairwell
head cocked
with one eye
i look down
with the other
keep
watch
for that which lusts
after my tender body

the world
is made of black and sun
pretty bars
made of light
of black
will I know
which is substance
for my pink toes to grab
which
surface
where I may peck

but these stairs
street
are so very empty
of half-buns
donut crumbs
spilled corn

and that advancing predator
front paws hidden
too
looks along

empty street
for half-buns
donut crumbs
my plump
feathered

hope

Then They Came Out

it was the summer of the rats
        homeless from roadwork   new-pipe laying
        water cut off
they came to drink from sprinklers
        feed on fallen bird seeds

some showed up sleek and brown
        but for the tail not unpretty
others   poisoned   grotesquely disproportioned
        green blood oozing
                squashed by passing cars
      or
              long yellow teeth exposed   sprawled on sidewalk

my friends   one swollen   from manufactured poppies   to ease her
        into a world i think she did believe in
            the other under plastic
                breathing only one element
      until no more

gods
        like us to rats
wanted them disappeared

        while scum   to surface risen
            live
                not to do away
        but to watch suffer
those who cannot   will not   eat   hunger-gnawed
        the pellets mockingly left out

Highway Song

quicksilver
runs
across
like sandaled
girls
these leaves
cottonwood
poplar
playing
blind-you
mirror
at edge
of concrete
car
tries
to eat
fast faster
to make it
end

above copses
guarded
by columns
of slender nymph
aspens
burly oaks
fraternity
of vultures
unraveling wings
glides
writing
on air
latest
obit

Open Ends

the wren house point of contention
as soon as I hung it
on the magnolia
sheltered wrens for three years
lay vacant
another
despite spring barrages
from sparrows in vain
trying to shove their bulk
through the Audubon-specified hole

in winter contorta tree's nakedness
revealed the threat—a hornets'
globe hanging like Christmas
so brilliantly wrought
it nearly kept me from destroying it

this year again
sparrows besieged the house
chickadees smarter
chipped at the hole
enough for them but not sparrows
went to it
waking me at dawn
disapproving *neh-eeh-eeh-eeh*

then
one summer day something like smoke
hung from the hole
compact mattress
I pulled
nothing in nest
not a sign

were they devoured silently
in the night
did they fledge
to remember
enchant with sweet calls
pierce when displeased
another spring?

Bird Secrets

you think you know
don't you
all about nests
how eggs lie shivering to the open skies
unless the bird sits
covering them

in the wrenhouse
chickadees set up home
        because we despite our arrogance
        and Audubon instructions
        on house building
can mostly wreck but not control
how other beings live

the next summer went by
house unused

i moved it thinking a jay
        or more likely hornets
        in their gorgeous pendant home nearby
had frightened the small birds

there it sat empty through another summer
        chickadees peering at opening
        flying away
        not to return

this fall i took it down
saw it full of stuffing
began with wire hook to clean it out
found
        among thickset moss   hair   cottonwool   milkweed silks
        packed more compactly soft than into any pillow
        protected
        as if in amniotic fluid

five dried-up eggs the size
of a child's fingernail

and understood
                    at last
the pall
        of death
these birds
            with brains no bigger than their eggs
            more wise than you and i
had sense
to flee from

Perfectly Clear

a clearing now
chickadee on stump
like the day's special on an old china plate
alert bewilderment

this space just yesterday
rustling   huge mobile   swinging city
            myriad lives
                     between and in the leaves   dancing bowl
                            the labyrinth beneath

a clearing
we call it
as the chickadee
looks
from knee level
for its heavens-scraping home

Rest Stop

        stunning my sight
        as if a decoy in his stillness
the red-tailed hawk on wire
        over the parking lot
        of this small park
watches

        a half an hour later
        returning from my walk
            no small birds to be seen in his vicinity
he preens
then returns to quietude

I watch
come closer
think I've startled him

for down he swoops
        on wings swishing open wider   more beautiful   than any fan
        on wings deploying in total silence
            as he lands
        I think
        on empty lawn
then see
him
        carrying away in talons
        limp black squirrel

can only
hope
death was as swift   as quiet
as that grace-clothed
descent

At Grass Level

a pink twist tie
worm authority stronger than any pope's
has wedded fescue
lanky   straight
with wild-maned dandelion
fast
indissolubly

until
robin's cocked eye
perceives
beak
tears
asunder

sending grass strand
into upright shock
curls to blow greyly
leaving head
as if a wig snatched off
small
bald

Mantis Shrimp

she looks goofy
        her eyes rolling in different directions
        all of her colored as if by a child trying out every purple shade in a new
                                                                                           box

her fists have her trapped under triple glass
        smaller than my pinky
        she packs the wallop of a .22-caliber bullet

how do I see her
        as she seeks privacy and the element of surprise

a flashing "smart" phone draws her out of her recess

I think
        if in the tank the phone
        would not be smart for long

Medusas

        from deeper waters they usually inhabit
        on these now perilous shores

unfold
        like passion flowers
                unlike them
        milky like foam
                unlike it
                      the texture of old glass in an old house

wavering windows
        to a green dense world
                not just green like jade
                      not like it
                            streaked with light
        fringed like a tasseled lampshade
                not like tassels
                      unless they be animated ruffles
        delicate pink
                like baby's blush
                      not like
                          unless a baby of molten alabaster

enfold
unfold
        the piping round undulating edges
                filled like syringe
                      but not contained
release
        not turning-to-stone
                but wishing-for-it
        writhing
        exquisite
pain

Sparrow's Fall

what you take to be
an understanding with a wild creature
means merely life is seeping out of it

as with the little sparrow
who hopped away under the cover of the yew
each time I caught her eating at the goldfinch feeder

humbly she left and humbly she returned
I looked away
then saw her—wing awry—hop only on the ground

next day the stupid dog
who couldn't find a bone if he tripped on it
found her and nearly toothless worried her to death

today a cluster of snowdrops lifts a massive clump
of sodden leaves two inches above ground
when dry they'll blow away

leaving these spears to pierce the air toward sun
until they split and drop their pearls small bells
pealing with silent laughter at their munificence

irish green wedded to delicately tinged
white blinding brilliance in this world
of drab small quiet deaths

Late Disturbances

cicadas chainsaw the dusk
on the racket ride

a consternation conjugation
constellation of starlings

arrowheads loosed from full quivers
all four points of the compass

targets — topmost tips of cottonwood
sugar maples

vibrate pierced to leaves' heart
undulant bathed

still in a light glossing
their burdens

while we already in dark
hear the swell

of ancient leaving song
by these master mimics

only pretending
to breach sky and time

only pretending to launch themselves
surge like gale winds

Heralds

        this november afternoon winking
                like a new shiny penny from the grass
alarm systems go off

        clothed in soot silk
crows crack open the mild air
the smaller birds take up sharp trills

against unruptured blue of this rare sky
        i see her
                outline incarnadine
hawkdeath
        planing
                indifferent   or so it seemed
        to all those large small cries
                at desolation sure to come

she soars
        in her fierce raiment
disappears toward sinking sun

jay atop the naked sycamore
will not give up
        unwilling to the last
                to bow
        to what
these arthritic leaves   surgery-altered trees   we
acquiesce

Wind Effect

in hurricane Sandy's winds
        here amid the Great Lakes attenuated by a thousand miles
                from that fierce whirlpool

birds blow like leaves
        wings torn backward

i watch them helpless
        blown   torn
              like leaves

We Decree

everything is just like us
the chestnut tree, the dancer
but think again

grow without legs
upside down
        hermaphrodite
        pubic hair purple magenta orange blue-white
        like snow at dawn
        perfumed musk damask lavender gardenia violet
offer to the wind and passing bugs
        streams of powdered sperm
        glue-covered cervix
        and treasure in the depths
                beside the point
                of pistil and of stamen
        opened for haired and feathered
        who pander for you as they drink
        your sweet

so when they say deadheading
they mean each time you close up
with sighs of petals
scattering, corolla folding in upon itself
like a mouth with no more teeth,
they mean they chop off green swelling, promise
of pod fruit nut punk crest of fluff
bearing carrying feeding
seed
they mean
you'll have to grow it all, the painted perfumed pubis
expose it all
to wind to passing chance
again again

So Much Depends

for Olivia (*pace William Carlos Williams*)

so much depends upon green caterpillars
       juicy with protein
              feeding blind nestlings
                    the stuff to clothe their nakedness
                            melting into a gory mess
                                  that feeds its revenant
          transcendent   (but not before devouring its former self)

so much depends upon the sideroad milkweed
       fat leaves   stalk full   of the unkindest poison
       pink flower clusters whoring the neighborhood
              making us all
                        drunk with fragrance

so much depends in each of these (to us) invisible links

upon our
staying
hand

ABOUT THE AUTHOR

Anca Vlasopolos has published over 200 poems, the poetry collections "Penguins in a Warming World" and "Walking Toward Solstice," and the non-fiction novel "The New Bedford Samurai," as well as the highly acclaimed memoir "No Return Address." She is Professor Emerita at Wayne State University, where she taught English and Comparative Literature for 39 years. She lives with her husband, Anthony Ambrogio, a writer and editor, in Centerville, MA